THEN TWEETS
MY SOUL

Published by Canon Press
P.O. Box 8729, Moscow, Idaho 83843
800.488.2034 | www.canonpress.com

Cover design by James Engerbretson.
Cover and interior illustrations by Susan Vednor.
Interior layout by James Engerbretson and Valerie Anne Bost.

Printed in the United States of America.

Library of Congress Cataloging-in-Publication Data is forthcoming.

16 17 18 19 20 21 22 23   12 11 10 9 8 7 6 5 4 3 2 1

THEN TWEETS
MY SOUL

The Best of the Church Curmudgeon

David Regier

canonpress
Moscow, Idaho

*This is dedicated to the wonderful woman
who has endured my humor with remarkable grace,
and to the benighted kids who have inherited it.*

THE INTRODUCTION

Meet the Church Curmudgeon

An Interview by David Regier

David Regier: So, uh, you're the guy who sits on the back pew, right?

Church Curmudgeon: Yes, left rear, farthest from the drums. I measured.

DR: What made you start tweeting in the first place?

CC: I did it to bring balance to the cyber-continuum. It was leaning toward young and dumb.

DR: I see. How has that been working out for you?

CC: Fool's errand. But I appear to be the man for the job.

DR: So you just gripe about your pet peeves in the church?

CC: That would be petty. Rather, I'm inviting people to dialogue about our shared journey.

DR: That sounds like a bit of a stretch.

CC: The way I see it, overcoming obstacles builds character. I am happy to be that obstacle.

DR: You sure pick on Baptists a lot. And Methodists. And Calvinists. And worship leaders.

CC: As an old pastor said, "The dog that yelps is the one you hit." He also said, "You never see a U-Haul behind a hearse." But that's neither here nor there.

DR: So you're an equal-opportunity Curmudgeon?

CC: My criticism is not free. But somehow, they all find a way to earn it.

DR: Are things really as bad as you say?

CC: It ain't the way it used to be, I'll tell you that.

THE TWEETS

They call it a "selfie" because "narcissistie" is too hard to spell.

Youth pastor fell asleep during morning session. We left clothes on our chairs, exited quietly. Then I blew a trumpet.

Pastor's on a Twitter fast. So he's going out and changing the church sign every half hour.

How do Calvinists set off their fireworks? Predetonation.

Worship team practice is canceled. Use the four chords from last week.

Jesus saved my soul. Peter's vision saved my bacon.

He's so Methodist, he goes to Sprinklin' Donuts.

You shouldn't be able to call your church "First Baptist" without there being some sort of playoff system.

Guest preacher this morning. As usual, Elmer and I are going to "Amen" him at odd times to throw him off his game.

Pastor wants you to have the passion for church that you have for the Super Bowl. Scream at him if he fumbles his words during the sermon.

Ever been to a homeschool girls' soccer game? The parents sound like they're screaming a sermon outline. Faith! Hope! Charity! GRAAAACE!

The parking ministry has issued an apology for tazing Miss Edna. Again, please make sure your sun shade does not obscure your handicapped sticker.

Q: How many Baptists does it take to change a light bulb in the sanctuary?

A: They can't. That would involve raising their hands in church.

———————

Know why the instruments always drop out on the 3rd chorus of the song?

Union rules. Except the drummer. He took his break on the 1st verse.

———————

Pastors and soccer fans are the only people who think that something with three points in an hour is exciting.

Here's a little test:

1. In winter it gets _____ outside.

If you were able to fill in the blank, stop acting surprised.

That veggie bacon exists is evidence of the fall.

That someone would serve it to the unsuspecting is evidence of total depravity.

The idea that all men are created equal loses everything if you believe that men were not created.

Do King-James-only churches post their sermons on ThouTube?

If you leave your Bible at church, we highlight all the really weird passages to make your children wonder about you when you die.

Think Mary ever gets tired of hearing singers ask if she knew?

———————————

If you don't take the bulletin, the greeter dies a little inside. Just so you know.

———————————

In the Old Testament, the choir led the army into battle.

Because the worship team looked ridiculous in their skinny jeans.

———————————

Christmas Eve was taken from the side of Christmas Adam.

Celebrate with a McRib.

I named my three steaks Shadrach, Meshach, and Abednego in hopes of a fourth showing up on the grill. But they all just came out raw.

Spiritual warfare is when you pass by a Chick-fil-A on a Sunday and just wish . . .

Our local atheist is suing to get it changed to just plain Zilla.

Worship leader was on fire again today. Hair gel and Advent candles don't mix.

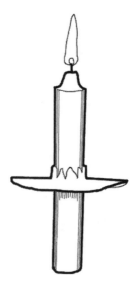

It's one thing to be at a loss for words in worship. It's another to write a song called "Jesus, I'm All, Like, Dude."

———————————

Nice to see thousands of young people using technology to land a man on the moon.

Oh, wait. You're taking pictures of your latte.

———————————

If the guitarist is raising his hands this morning, he's not overcome in worship.

He just doesn't know the chords in the Christmas song.

Q: How many angels can dance on the head of a pin?

A: Dancing's a sin, so zero.

———————————

Please pray for the children's director, who fell off a ladder and suffered injuries to her head & shoulders, knees & toes, knees & toes.

———————————

I know God chooses the foolish things of the world, but you don't have to jump to the front of the line by wearing those skinny pants.

Since everybody just stares at their phones and quotes famous pastors anyway, this year we're holding a men's retweet.

———————————

We eliminated the announcements during the service. Nobody will know what's going on, but we'll beat the Methodists to the Golden Corral.

———————————

Nice when the sound man plays MP3s of the worship songs after the service so we can hear what they were supposed to sound like.

If we really wanted to be seeker-friendly, we'd forget the coffee and put in a bacon bar.

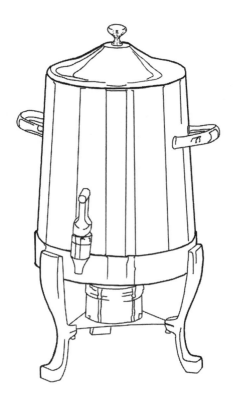

Why are so few soccer players Calvinists?

They hardly ever make five points.

———————————

Love it when the youth pastor preaches. Don't get his jokes, his haircut, or his point, but he's done in 23 minutes.

———————————

Q: Know why God doesn't want Baptists to dance?

A: Ever watched a Baptist dance?

———————————

If the pastor sees his shadow when he pokes his head out of his study, we'll have six more weeks of this sermon series.

―――――――――

Due to our inability to find VBS clean-up volunteers, tomorrow's wedding will be jungle-themed.

―――――――――

Business tip: If you're starting a Christian clothing line, probably best not to call it "Cross Dressing."

―――――――――

Whoever said Baptists don't gamble never had to choose from six potato salads at a potluck.

World War II would have ended much more quickly if the generals could have read all these leadership quotes on Twitter.

———————

Oh good, the Grammy Awards. Our annual national reminder that this country needs a butt whooping and a haircut.

———————————

Ushers are giving out "man cards" this morning. If you're wearing skinny jeans, we'll just take them right back.

———————————

Worship band practice suddenly got quiet. Somebody must have slipped them some sheet music.

———————————

Like there's ever been a drummer who'd be satisfied playing "pa-rum-pa-pum-pum" for three and a half minutes.

———————

Today is Pentecost Sunday. As always, ushers are standing by in case anything gets weird.

———————

If you don't think God is patient, forgiving, and long-suffering, consider that He has read ALL of Twitter.

———————

Referring to your wife as smokin' hot means something else entirely if she has passed away.

———————

I may not be able to explain the Trinity using donuts, but it's worth a few tries.

———————

Our pastor has dreams of feeding 5,000, but mostly he just loafs and fishes.

———————

My pastor's mishandling of Greek is enough to make an Aorist tense.

Our church has always had women in combat. It's called the decorating committee.

If the worship leader sees his shadow Sunday, there will be six extra repetitions of each chorus.

———————

You know it's time to talk to the tech guy when the screen says:

OLMG, when I in awesome wonder . . .

———————

Funny how none of the ancient hymns sound as dated as "Lord, I Lift Your Name on High."

———————

Our drummer hasn't seen many dangers or toils, but he's sure gone through a lot of snares.

―――――――――

Hired the church drummer to help with my garden, but it's not working out.

He keeps dropping fat beets.

―――――――――

Apparently, the truths we hold to be self-evident need to be explained to some people again.

―――――――――

In an effort to be more biblically correct, they are painting millions of bodies under the ark in the nursery.

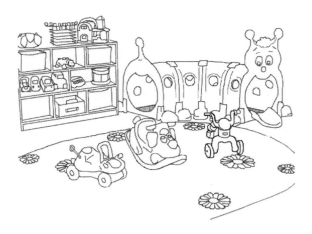

The King James is very hard to understand, but u hav no prblm rdng ths lol rofl smh

---

If you call Mary the Mother of God, then logically, you have to call Elizabeth the Auntie Christ.

———————————

Saturday's All-Day Men's Event will focus on how to spend more time with your family.

———————————

I know this is odd, but I took a picture of someone else today. I call it a "someone elsie."

———————————

When my pastor's discouraged, I've always found that a note reminding him how to do his job helps me feel better.

———————————

Putting the healthy vegan lady in charge of the men's breakfast was the worst idea since contemporary Christian music.

———————————

When your pastor says he wants you to respond to the text during the sermon, he's not talking about your phone.

———————————

Even if your drummer's short and keeps good time, it's improper to call him the MetroGnome.

———————————

Worship team practice tonight. Those four chords aren't going to learn themselves, you know.

———————————

They kicked the guitarist off the worship team, and won't let him come back until he finds Gsus.

———————————

2/3 of all church plants fail within the first year.

That's why we switched to plastic ones. Don't have to water them.

Tried planting some flowers in leftover mashed potatoes. Up from the gravy, a rose.

————————

The warm breeze you feel against your face is just the handbasket picking up speed. No cause for alarm.

————————

My generation: To the moon with slide rules & protractors.

Yours: Can't get out of McDonald's drive-thru without GPS.

Imagine what Acts 2 could have been like if they'd had lasers and fog machines.

———————

I must say, the Grammys did put up a powerful argument against intelligent design.

———————

New charismatic megachurch in town. They call it PenteCostco.

———————

It would be easier for the congregation to lip-sync if they'd put the right words up.

Choosing a movie is easy these days. All you have to do is decide which aspect of your spiritual character you'd like destroyed.

———————

Just got the new Worship Leader Study Bible.

Repeats the last verse of each chapter 7 times.

Used to look at *National Geographic* for strange piercings, clothing, and tattoos. Now I just look at the worship team.

Hate it when I fall asleep in Sunday school class. Now I'll be up through the whole sermon.

Tech team is installing new software to make the words come up more quickly after we sing them.

Worship band's practicing. This Sunday, it may be best to go ahead and let the rocks cry out.

I'm going to write a manual for church audio techs.

I'm calling it *Sound Doctrine*.

Silly Adventists! The one denomination that can go to Chick-fil-A after church, and they're vegetarians.

Instead of Sunday School we call it a Fantasy Doctrine League so the men will do their homework.

———————

Sorry worship leader. The only time I clap is if I want the lights on.

———————

No, I will not high-five you tomorrow. #PalmSunday

———————

If you try to deceive people by using a hairpiece, there will be hell toupee.

Worship team practice tonight. They'll be working on new arrangements of old hymns so the seniors can hate them too.

Had a dream that the pastor preached about this beard fad.

Hundreds came forward and asked, "What must I do to be shaved?"

Stricter children's check-in procedures began today. Seven parents "lost" their tags.

Looks like we're starting an orphanage.

The tech booth has more computing power than it took to land men on the moon.

It'd be nice if they could get the words to match the song.

Thought I grabbed a chocolate chip cookie.

But was raisin. It was raisin indeed.

NASCAR doesn't hold a candle to the Baptists and Methodists racing to Cracker Barrel.

Let him who is without donuts cast the first scone.

The blended service is where we all take turns getting ticked off.

They should call a seminary graduation "Casting out the DMins."

Jesus gave his disciples fish for breakfast. I'm really glad that never became a thing.

———————————

I'm of the opinion that "veggie bacon" should be classified as hate speech.

———————————

Pastor set a goal of 15 new church plants this year. Probably mostly ferns.

———————————

His Starbuck's® order had more words in it than the worship song he led on Sunday.

It will be easy to pick out this generation in heaven, because they'll all be staring at their empty phone hand.

Jesus can turn water into wine.

But a Methodist can turn wine into Welch's®.

I hope Twitter is printing this all out somewhere so future archaeologists can tell how our culture fell apart.

I'm just like Moses.

I get angry when I show up and find people serving de caf.

If the feeding of the five thousand had been at the end of the book of Acts, it could have been done with bacon.

They spend $200K on a crystal-clear sound system. The guitarist buys a distortion pedal.

If you advertise your ice cream as "hand-scooped", would that make it a Palm Sundae?

Worship team practice is starting late. Drummer lost track of time. Usually doesn't do that until he starts playing.

Service Project: The youth group will be ripping new jeans to send to uncool kids in third-world countries.

FYI: Putting your NCAA bracket in the giving envelope does NOT give you a chance to win the offering.

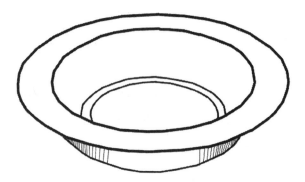

If you ditch the Scripture reading and prayer, you'll have time for another awesome worship song with 8 words in it.

Those hailstones are tears, frozen and hurled angrily from heaven by your late English teacher who saw you write "could of."

Before the internet, it took much more effort to get upset about things we had no idea existed. You kids have it easy.

Pastors: Context is key. "My calves are killing me!" means one thing at the gym, another in a barn.

———————————

Our worship team's arrangement of the National Anthem was apparently written by Francis Off Key.

———————————

Power corrupts. Absolute power corrupts absolutely. Then there's the church wedding coordinator.

———————————

Everyone fell asleep during Heads Bowed Eyes Closed, including the pastor. Lutherans beat us to Cracker Barrel.

———————————

Colorado marijuana taxes add up to around 29%. If you think that's high, you should see the taxpayers.

———————————

The sanctuary is quiet. The service is about to begin. Every head is bowed, sending one last tweet.

———————————

Those cold winds are the icy stares of hymn writers past who have had their third verses skipped. Again.

Hobby Lobby is grown up now, and would prefer you to refer to it as Hobert Lobert.

"Here I raise mine Ebenezer."

—Scrooge's mom

If our creepy puppet ministry saves one creepy kid, it will be worth it all.

I think the young people are speaking in tongues. What's a venty mocky auto?

Knowledge travels at the speed of light. But it can't keep up with stupid.

Singles' Ministry got mad last year when we had them serve at the Valentine's Banquet. So this year we're letting them stay in the kitchen.

———————————

Deacons cut 25% from the music budget, so the worship leader's down to 3 chords now.

———————————

My pastor is praying that church will go back to the way it used to be. He has to. I put it on the prayer card.

———————————

Don't tell pastor! We just installed a Sleep Number® Pew in the back row. Mine's a 78.

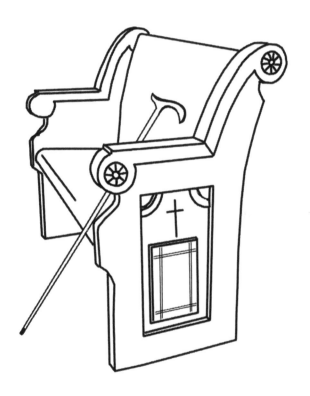

How come no one came to the Calvinist pastor's birthday party?

No invitation.

Asked a Methodist if he sprinkles coffee on his donut. He asked me if I dunk my pancake.

"Peter, what's that body spray you're using?"

"Well, Bartholomew, it's called 'Axe of the Apostles.'"

You know it's going to be a good cantata when the Homeschool Separatist Handbell Choir shows up with a fog machine.

———————————

They're taking down the LCD "parent alert" thing in the sanctuary, because the toddlers can just call them on their smart phones.

———————————

Good King Wenceslas looked out
On the feast of Stephen
Saw the shoppers all about
"Guys, I just. can't. even."

That song "The Circle of Life" isn't about donuts. But it should be.

Too much sodium can kill you. Remember Lot's wife.

Again, just because you cantata, doesn't mean you shouldtata.

May your praises today be holier than the worship leader's jeans.

Nothing was really that great before it. Nothing's been that great since. Sliced bread was pretty much the pinnacle.

The same people incapable of understanding "Thee" or "Thou" in a hymn hav no prblm figrng out a twt lik dis.

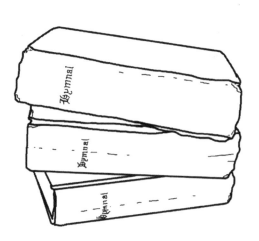

You're a theology geek if you hear "pair of cleats" and think about the Holy Spirit.

———————————

When they named it the World Wide Web, they failed to tell us that we were the flies, not the spiders.

———————————

The church air conditioner broke, so please turn to your neighbor and give them a cold glare instead of a warm welcome.

———————————

A guy got caught stealing an idol from our local museum in hopes of auctioning it off. Baal has been set at $50,000.

———————————

If there is a purgatory for worship leaders, it will be a million years spent singing the third verses of the hymns.

———————————

If you sing "O For a Thousand Tongues to Sing" at a megachurch, it's like you're wishing it were smaller.

———————————

I love how people who mock the Bible for having food laws change their whole diet on the basis of a Facebook link.

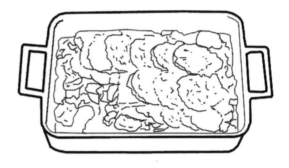

The Sunday School class on Hyper-Calvinism has been cancelled due to unforeseen circumstances.

When the guitarist raises his hands and closes his eyes, either he's really worshipping or the song is in E flat.

————————————

I tried to cancel my meeting with Hank from the King-James-only church, but he didn't receptus my textus.

————————————

Technology has advanced to the point where all the stupidity in the world can be instantly delivered to your phone.

————————————

We need an app that gathers tens of thousands of people together in stadiums for evangelistic meetings. #InstaGraham

———————————

Cleaning up after the preschool riot. Guess we'll never buy the off-brand goldfish again.

———————————

Worship practice is wrapping up. All that's left is for the tech team to put the lyrics through the slide randomizer.

———————————

When I was a boy, the universe was 2.5 billion years old. Now it's more than 13 billion. No wonder my joints hurt.

Those who fail to learn from history are condemned to drag the rest of us through it again, kicking and screaming.

If you're going to offer a long prayer to open the men's breakfast, please pray that the eggs get hot again.

If your church needs black coffee, don't preach a Vanilla Frappuccino.

Worship leader's going to explain to the seniors why he doesn't do hymns. Or, "Singer in the Hands of an Angry Mob."

———————

According to the youth pastor, video game time with students counts as "discipleship" as long as they don't cuss.

———————

A church across town just hired some freak worship leader with no tattoos or piercings.

———————

Hard to take polls seriously considering they only get data from people who don't mind being interrupted during dinner.

————————

Worship leader tip: Asking for a "clap offering" is a way of telling Jesus you're sorry the song didn't go well.

————————

Jacob: *sneezes*

Isaac: Bless you!

Esau: *sneezes*

Isaac: *shrugs*

Ministry Update: We got 13 people to join the committee in charge of finding 4 nursery workers.

Everyone deserves respect and tolerance.

Whoever doesn't believe that needs to be isolated, shamed, and rejected.

Powerful sermon at the seminary graduation. Even the DMins believed, and trembled.

The church cut the seniors' group budget to 20 bucks per event. So tonight we're going to party like it's $19.99.

And Jesus said, "Go to the conference and listen to bands and speakers until you are clothed with power from on high."

Would the first-time visitors please stand as we welcome you with a moment of awkward silence?

If I speak with the tongues of men and angels, but have not love, I sound like our drummer on the third chorus of every song.

Is anyone else troubled by Linus's seasonal wavering between Christianity and pagan pumpkin worship?

The youth pastor went to 4 years of Bible college so he could learn to say "What does that verse mean to you?"

———————————

Take your mom to Chick-fil-A for Mother's Day. One more disappointment won't hurt.

———————————

Printing an order of service might make us miss the Holy Spirit, but the right music and lighting cues make Him show up.

———————————

I thought we defeated the Grammar Nazis in Word War To.

You heard about the soloist whose laryngitis was cured by communion juice.

Just a singer, saved by grapes.

Worship leaders, if you keep making that face when you sing, it will stay like that in heaven.

———————————

Worship leader's at a conference to learn how to rearrange the same seven words, only louder & with fewer chords.

———————————

Drummer got called out of town, won't be at church tomorrow. The prayer of a righteous man availeth much.

———————————

No visitors at church today. Guess we need to trim our hedge of protection.

———————————

Worship band killed it this morning, if by "it" you mean the dwindling joy of my twilight years.

———————————

Our youth group will be leaving Instagram this week for a short-term mission trip to Facebook.

———————————

You know you're a Baptist when you start examining your conscience every time you get a whiff of Welch's®.

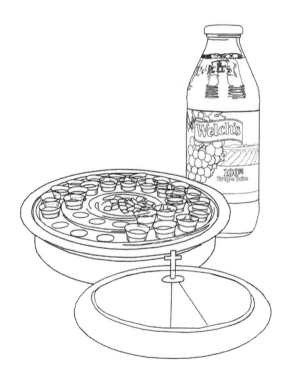

Mary glared at him, pa rum pa pum pum.
Him and his drum.

Coexist. Or else.

Whoever serves me veggie bacon out of
concern for my longevity is obviously not
concerned about his own.

That verse about a day being like a
thousand years is a prophecy fulfilled by
the DMV.

If I were an astronaut, right before the launch I'd tell my wife, "Honey, I just need some space right now."

———————————

Usually when the writing is on the wall, it portends the death of a culture. But hey, fine, throw out the hymnals and use a projector.

———————————

Pastor left his iPad just sitting here . . . . Think I'll set his sermon notes on "shuffle."

———————————

We told you that you could grow up to be anything. We weren't expecting so many to choose "weirdo."

———————————

The realistic novel as an art form will be dead in six years, as every third sentence will have to be, "He glanced at his phone."

———————————

Note to converts: if your phone gets baptized with you, it won't have eternal life.

———————————

Stay tuned for my choral musical about the Lion King of Judah.

Hakuna Cantata.

Our church buys the plastic ware "variety packs" for potlucks. Current kitchen total: 0 forks, 23 spoons, 137,563 knives.

Drove past the atheist church again. Their live nativity has a bunch of people lined up at a microscope.

———————

Our XTREME ministry is witnessing while skydiving today. Praying they don't make an impact.

———————

Candy makers: "Fun" is not a size.

———————

All the cool chipmunks are Alvinists.

Then there was the lady who skipped one phrase of the Lord's Prayer because it contained gluten.

———————————

Interesting how energy drinks didn't become a thing until people did nothing but use their thumbs.

———————————

I forget the words to that song we sang. Is it "Yes Lord yes Lord yes yes Lord" or "Yes yes Lord yes yes Lord yes Lord"?

———————————

Those red numbers are a nursery alert? I thought they were rating the pastor's sermon points.

Substitute preacher! Everybody switch seats!

A choice lay before Boaz: be merciful, or be Ruthless.

———————————

Pastor is praying that the worship band would leave and an organist would show up.

He has to. I put that on the prayer card, too.

———————————

If a sinner repents before the end of the sermon, is it a two-point conversion?

———————————

You keep talking about law vs. gospel. Is that like the Gaithers' bus getting pulled over?

———————————

Today's worship songs give a broad range of self-expression to people who know seven words and like to repeat them.

———————————

Youth group service project: Distributing energy drinks at the nursing home. They all look so tired.

———————————

We hired an organist from the local baseball team.

The best part was getting a seventh inning stretch 2/3 of the way through the sermon.

———————————

New Testament word studies are all Greek to me, to Koine phrase.

———————————

Wrote a curriculum that sums up the two factions in our children's ministry. "You are the most special person in the universe. Now repent!"

They said to bring things we didn't want anymore to the youth garage sale fundraiser.

So I brought the church's drums.

Today, in an effort to be more accurate, the tech team is just going to type in what they think we're singing as we go.

———————————

Homeschool lockdown drill is over. You can come out of your room.

———————————

"Hymnals make you look down during worship."

—Guy who spends 70% of the time staring at his phone during the service.

———————————

Love the way pastor's eyes light up when he finds details in the Hebrew text that were missing in the Veggie Tales version.

———————————

Most of these modern worship song-writers could use a swift kick in the Fanny J. Crosby.

———————————

We need an executive order creating a constitutional amendment that makes things that are against the law illegal.

———————————

I won the drawing at seniors' lunch. I get to write next Sunday's anonymous criticism of the worship leader!

Was kind of expecting the person who took my favorite donut to go forward at the invitation. Obviously a hardened heart.

Nobody ever seems to give up college basketball for Lent.

———————————

Bible says we won't be tempted beyond what we can handle, but then I see someone with a selfie stick and I want to whack him with it.

———————————

I resolved not to eat any more donuts this year.

Of course, I won't eat any less donuts, either.

That cold wind is the icy stare of Johannes Gutenberg listening to you complain about how slow your Bible software is.

———————

Pastor, we'd like you to lead the "Making the Most of Your Family Time" study on Monday nights, since that's the only one you have free.

———————

If you don't like one of my jokes, treat it like the worship leader treats the 3rd verse of a hymn. Skip it & move on.

———————

Turns out Amos wasn't planking. Services will be Friday.

––––––––––––––––––

Shirt untucked, 3 days unshaven, hair sticking up:

Pastor = Relevant

Me = Nursing home escapee

––––––––––––––––––

Stupid cockroaches. The second you turn on the light, they scatter like potential nursery workers.

––––––––––––––––––

Hate it when I lose my dentures in the couch. That kind of thing can come back to bite you in the butt.

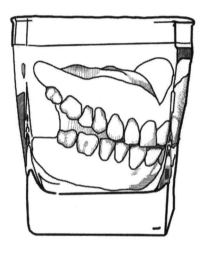

It used to be that the pastor's wife was huge and the sanctuary was smokin' hot.

———————

Seniors' study today: Dealing With Change—Becoming the Obstacle That God Wants You to Be.

———————————

The prayer of a righteous man availeth much, until he announceth it on social media.

———————————

The best thing about homeschool graduations is only having to listen to the first four notes of "Pomp and Circumstance."

———————————

The book of Acts is about the early church.

For you young people, that doesn't mean the 8:00 service.

U wdnt spel lik dis if ur tchr had smack ur hand wit a rulr lik she shold hav.

There was a small fire at the Methodist Church Sunday. The sprinklers went off.

Everyone was saved.

Worship team practice is cancelled tonight. The leader emailed out sheet music to a hymn and the guitarist exploded.

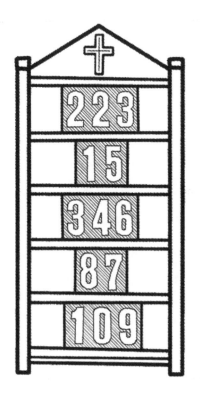

Hmm. My grocery bag says it's made of 80% unread bulletin inserts.

Worship team practice will be "unplugged" tonight. About halfway through. By me.

Q: How many dispensationalists does it take to replace a light bulb?

A: The new light bulb is not replacing the old, whose promises remain.

Saul consulted a medium.

David killed an extra-large.

_____

Caught a grown man sticking gum under the pew; had to take him to the back. There's a reason they call it the cry room.

_____

Ah, there's my pastor in the coffee shop. Think I'll go tell him a long, rambling, disconnected story.

_____

The grass withers,
the flower falls,
but the announcement time lasts forever.
Selah

Postmodernism took root in churches during the '90s, when they tried to simultaneously hold the ideas of "excellence" and "drama team."

I know Solomon said there's nothing new under the sun. Then again, he hadn't seen the worship leader's haircut.

One day, Christ will make every enemy a footstool for His feet. Too bad the name "Ottoman Empire" has already been taken.

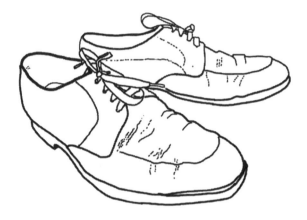

They wanted a photo of us raising our hands for the church website, so they took a picture of us approving the budget.

YOLOLO—You only laugh out loud once.

I wonder if Benny Hinn's dog knows how to heel.

Did I tell you about the time I brought my pig to the Pentecostal butcher? His leg got cured.

Thank God I'm not like those judgmental people.

Giving a man a half a donut is like telling him half his sins are forgiven.

In the war on obesity, I'm fighting for the side that has the gravy.

Putting speakers in the restrooms does not count as multi-site.

Pastor asked me to offer the prayer before tomorrow's message. Considering "Now I lay me down to sleep . . . "

If you take the pins out of the map in the foyer, the missionaries get raptured.

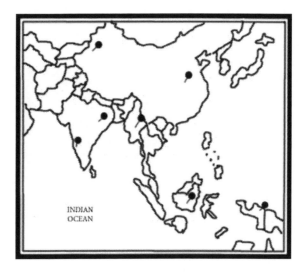

The worship leader wants to symbolize the Trinity, so each song this week has three chords.

We're hosting a heck house that will put the fear of gosh in you.

———————————

You've got to give props to the drama team.

———————————

The minute you have to say you're relevant, guess what?

———————————

Catholics have more children; Protestants have more sects.

So was Noah in charge of everything himself, or was there some sort of hierarky-arky?

———————————

For Pastor Appreciation Month, we bought him a plaque listing the ways he could do his job better.

———————————

There is no "I" in team.

Unless it's the worship team, and then it's every other word.

———————————

I may not agree with your choice of worship music, but I'll defend to the death your right to stop playing it.

I finally figured out that they're repeating the last chorus ten times to let the slides catch up.

All these Bible studies say they will Change. Your. Life. It just takes one committee meeting to Change. It. Back.

I washed the car this morning. So my eye is on the sparrow. And I know he's watching me.

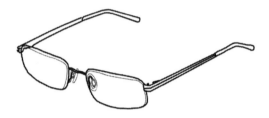

Sure, padded pews are nice, but the Hot Wheels don't roll the way they used to.

———————

Don't tell your folks it's a nursing home; say it's the senior ministry lock-in.

We're having a special outreach for Palm Sunday.

Bring a frond.

The worship leader doesn't think people understand the "Ebenezer" verse. He must think we're as dumb as a pile of rocks.

We told them to follow their dreams.

Unfortunately, none of those dreams included doing an honest day's work.

The line item for duct tape in the children's ministry budget looked high, until I remembered the Smith boys.

Headed over to the seminary barbecue this afternoon. Otherwise known as casting a pig into a herd of DMins.

The problem with "Every head bowed, every eye closed" is remembering to wake up when he says "Amen."

Blowout deals on hymns at How Great Thou Mart.

This morning's coffee was like our deacon board. Weak, bitter, and cheap.

You keep on talking about engaging the culture, but you act like you two are already married.

———————————

If you have to tell people "God gave me this song" to get them to listen to it, it may be that He didn't want it.

———————————

In case you were wondering, I'll be at Edna's today. She made her upyonder rolls. And, well, you know . . .

———————————

The worship leader asked how everyone was doing so the sound man gave him some feedback.

Moses raised his staff and divided a great sea. Our pastor raised one little issue and divided his staff.

First day of VBS, and I got 3 kids to rededicate themselves to staying off the lawn.

Working on my new seniors' Bible study, "Finding a Biblical Mandate to Justify Your Nostalgic Preferences."

Drama team's depicting sorry state of the arts in church. That's not what the skit's about, but they're sure depicting it.

The kingdom of heaven is like a mustard seed that, when you put it in the church fridge, turns into 47 bottles of mustard.

Children's church re-enacted the feeding of the five thousand, except with the flu.

No one can hold a candle to our worship leader's new hairstyle.

Much as we'd like to.

We're moving the cry room to the basement. That way we can call it the whine cellar.

I bet the Lone Ranger gets all choked up when they sing "More Precious Than Silver."

Parking Ministry has been renamed to Parking Militia. Stay out of the visitors' spaces Sunday.

At Pentecost, tongues of fire rested on the disciples' heads. The room's sprinkler system was clearly not up to code.

———————

You know she's a visitor when she yells "Bingo!" after the last blank on the sermon outline.

———————

They're installing the new youth pastor today. As with any installation, he's missing a few important screws.

———————

If you see me wearing an ephod, I'm just doing it to be Aaronic.

Pastor looks refreshed after his vacation. We'll have to work on that this week.

———

58580449R00069

Made in the USA
Lexington, KY
13 December 2016